Lemons & Lessons in Love

Nicky Taylor

BookLeaf Publishing

India | USA | UK

Presentation by *BookLeaf Publishing*

Web: www.bookleafpub.com

E-mail: info@bookleafpub.com

ISBN: 9789358312560

First edition 2023

ACKNOWLEDGEMENT

Thank you to BookLeaf Publishing for giving me this opportunity as a budding writer.

Golden Kitchen

I want to live in a home with a kitchen
where my May bells bloom --
They sit in the gold of the sun in the window and
each blossom for you.
Pray to sing in a home with a kitchen, where we
dance to a holy tune;
Settle down by the tableside and eat a meal for
two.
Wish to live in a home with a kitchen where you
hear me swell and swoon, and at night, while we
gaze into the stars you whisper and tell me I am
the moon.

I finish your cold table scraps --
you scratch my back in the yellowed hue.
I'll always be your last bite, as long as I'm with
you.
You didn't make me a different person,
the common refrain of lovers in our favorite
shows.
There was a part of me I was scared to live as,
and now that part glows.

Rot

The constant ringing ears of being head over
heels,
a migraine that comes with pining,
it never leaves my thoughts.

The contradictory mutualistic parasite,
beautiful orchids bloom
from the brain stem.

Roots grow from my soles
as I stand enamored, perhaps terrified,
frozen by the threat of beauty in pain.

Seychelles

Become the fizz in my drink when I need a lift --
pinching pennies for a dinner or two.
Just sitting in an empty lot clears the mist --
I feel full doing nothing with you.

I am gloriously in love with you;
Stars are in love with dust and time.
Every drop of water needs its glass
paired with a hint of lime.

Strawberry Fig Newton

"The phone goes both ways,"
and yet I still didn't call.

I forget what your face looks like,
and didn't remember your voice until today.
Your calloused hands would brush my hair;
Would you still hug me the same way?

I feel I am a puppy in a baby's bassinet --
small and protected; out of place and element.
Ensconced in all that is innocent.
Who else would remember my dog house but
you?

Reverence in Motion

Selfless worship for you and I;
we are designed by which we revere.
Carved from holiness, we live in a world
with our love in mind, my dear.

I didn't think I could live in this place,
a lucky fate surrounds my every thought.
You are every fear, and want, and reality --
Everything I have ever sought.

The Figure Eight Incident

Face heats up over the scuffed permafrost
surface.
A stranger sees tears in their eyes.
Shaking, balanced on blades, surrounded by
slices into ice. Her hands are outstretched --
the blocked path creates a new life
in the palms of her frosted gloves.
Fingers entangle as force grows;
wind and passion pushes them into the wall.
The strangers are safe in each others arms.
Laughs are exchanged; they will
never see each other again.

Reflections of Her

The stained glass girl; light passes through her
skin.
She refracts color on a white canvas
and paints our fresh white wall.
The stained glass girl; but God she sees through
me.
She seems to be looming,
those colors of carnival.

Her reflection shatters my soul,
yet I give all that I've got
in her ornamented arms;
With the stained glass girl,
I live 'til I rot.

Warmth fades those hues;
dust coats her fingers
whilst hairline fractures
make their way into my mind.

The reflection of lovers past is a nauseating sight
when one is not ready
for the shades in the light.

At Least You Have the Bathroom Floor

Systems present to protect
to lock those away

A way to keep each other safe
from each other

Will there never be a day of safety
within this padlocked home?

Pipe Dream

She has just stopped at a café,
the one off of highway sixteen.
Coming home from her teaching job,
a kiss and a coffee. A book on the counter.
"I love you," in a café,
that is home.

SKY (Never Understood Church as a Child)

Maybe if I keep using religion as a deliverance
it will get old and worn; My holy love
will seem less pious,
but rather beautiful in the sickening way.

The way mold seeps into wood
and dandelions grow through the floorboards.
The way rocks shatter stained glass murals,
thrown from soft hands and dirty nails.

Will you still care for my texts
when all that is left
is crumbled at the foundation?
I shall care for you like I was built to.

Perhaps we were built for more
than just devotion in our hollowed halls --
How dear is the silence
of love in peace.

Burnt Pasta

Three words wrecked this reality
and it will never be I love you;
it will never be I miss you or please don't go,
don't leave me or anything we want.

I don't know.
You didn't know?
Communication from a cotton mouth
to a soap filled maw --
into our static filled minds, there is
no translation.

And it's a tragic pattern I've woven for myself,
may those words be the punchline
next in line
for someone else's demise
And may no one laugh when you are done.

Grieving What Hasn't Gone

Got into bed and ripped off my clothes,
sobbed until the sheets were worn.
They are wet
tears falling over nothing falling over
nothing at all.

I feel broken over nothing at all,
dry heaving in the thoughts
of you going away.
I am nothing at all anymore.

Should I feel prepared now
that I've gotten a
taste of your absence?
Or will it feel worse

than I could ever comprehend?
I couldn't remember
the last thing I had said to you.
So now the first thing

I say is, "I missed you,"
and, "I love you,"
and, "Please, don't
leave again."

Koi Ponds

The hand sewn dresses got
loved by dirt in our yard, which
ended up caked in my hair
and our lives.

Trees were cut down, though I didn't
understand why
Cherries fell to the ground, through
the sieve you designed.

The smartest woman I know,
with the mind of a Draco
and an author who never was.

Gratitude isn't
something to be overstated,
especially when others
are watching and waiting.

I love you,
thank you,
and please keep telling me
about your books.

LIT DEVICES

How I obsess over the metaphor.
You are my mashed potatoes and my peaches;
the song I need to hear and the gloves I forgot.
You're my new home, my new life.

How I am endeared to the simile --
you're like an embrace to me,
& I love you as one loves breathing.

I love being in love with being in love with you.

Recess for Worms

Two girls have just come home -- one from a bus
full of screaming and stress; the other with her
mom
asking if everything went okay.

They both go outside
and play in the mud
With worms that ate dirt
from the same Earth each morning.

Two girls stare in the mirror -- covered in
pictures from prom night; each throwing darts
into their thighs.

They laugh walking down
the pavement
Picking up worms and returning
them to this beautiful world.

Mini Me

Most women are survived by their daughters.
Most daughters survive by their sins.
And is it that uncanny, the harsh cut of a scream followed
by handfuls of hair in the sink?
I wished I could wrap my hands around our throat,
breathing for the first time.

Those things in front of the mirror -- wraps and powders and shakes
designed for a sense of dread that hasn't yet been invented --
I lie under the desk and lay in your embrace,
waiting for a day to be free.
Until one day, I woke up, and I was.

Things are good now -- I am the daughter and son you always wanted.
Though perhaps I wasn't needed.
I love you more than words and
vengeful cycles have come to an end.

I am sorry for everything that came between us
even more so for what brought us together.

Pain and torture for nothing more than a few
days spent,
but sometimes that is all we can take.

Thank you for everything that has happened in
this life --
may the next be beautiful before the inevitable
strikes.

Beasts

Eyes bigger than any thoughts,
just love and warmth inside of you.
Food motivated by instincts
you will never be aware of.

We watch birds all day --
me to unwind and you
for the hunger that
you've never suffered.

You sleep endlessly --
Work lasts hours, day and night,
and you bounce from rest to wake
as if it is your job.

The best creation put on this planet was you:
A friend in the form of
joyous fur.

Quantum Mechanics

You are more than just
a light --
you are the very concept of color
and everything I need to see.

A star light-years away
with your hands in mine.
He is bright, and he is here,
and he is all mine.

113-209

Critics will never see the most beautiful
art because only I can see
your eyes from this angle
and feel this texture on your back --

No audiophile experiences the best
song of this lifetime
that is your fingers tapping the table
or you singing to yourself as you drive.

A part of me wishes that this
love is something unique
to us --
but it makes me feel so happy

A part of me wishes
everyone else feels it too.

Observations of a Cog

Doing the thing
we all hate most
has helped me meet the
best of Strangers.

A little girl told me, today,
she wanted to
be like me when she grew up.
All I could think

was to panic. And so,
I told her to
be kind and
never grow up
instead.

Fruit Basket

We are all just fruit in a
culinary kitchen. Sweet and
sour, paired together
for what is best.

When one starts to rot,
we all follow suit. Fresh thoughts
follow the sugar sprinkled
on my flesh.

A bitter lemon goes
best with a
slice of peach
in our glass.